RISE UP AND WALK

40 Day Devotional to Lift You Above
What Holds You Down

by Kim Ordile

A note from Mary Glaser:
I have a personal interest in this book
by Kim (Kenyon) Ordile. Kim's mother
Carol Kauffman Kenyon was a cousin
of my late husband Marvin Glaser.
(Carol's mother Sylvia Bebb Kauffman
and Marvin's mother Vesta Bebb Glaser
were sisters.)
In November of 2020, Kim will be 54
years old. She has been dealing with
ALS since October of 2012.

Published by:
TIME IN THE DESERT, LLC,
7210 Virginia Parkway, Unit 6736, McKinney, Texas 75071
www.timeinthedesert.com

1st Edition

Copyright © 2018 by Kim Ordile
Edited by Kelli Sallman

Scriptures taken from the Holy Bible, New International Version®, NIV®. Copyright © 1973, 1978, 1984, 2011 by Biblica, Inc.™ Used by permission of Zondervan. All rights reserved worldwide. *www.zondervan.com* The "NIV" and "New International Version" are trademarks registered in the United States Patent and Trademark Office by Biblica, Inc.™

ISBN: 978-0-9988494-4-7   *ebook*
          978-0-9988494-2-3   *paperback*
          978-0-9988494-3-0   *hardcover*

Co-Published by:

Division of Human Improvement Specialists, llc.
WWW.HISPUBG.COM | *info@hispubg.com*

Dedicated to Louis, Joseph, and Jessa.

May God bless you above and beyond all
you could ever ask or think.

Contents

Preface

As Kim's husband, ministry partner, and caretaker, I want to take a moment to share a little bit about Kim. Today she sits in an electric wheelchair, unable to walk. She can no longer reach out her hands to touch someone or grab a bottle of water. She has lost the ability to speak with her voice. Though she is still able to eat, she takes liquids through a PEG tube and uses a breathing machine at intervals during the day to increase her oxygen levels. In spite of all these handicaps, she lights up every room she enters. The joy in her heart is contagious. She views her disability with ALS as a blessing from the Lord. Granted, she would like to be healed. But her greater desire is to be close to God. You can see this aspiration in her writing.

Kim loves Jesus with all her heart, soul, mind, and strength. She placed her faith in Christ Jesus at the early age of five, two years before her father accepted Christ. Ever since, she has shared the love of Jesus with others. Throughout her school years, she lived for Jesus no matter how different, weird, or awkward she felt, or what others thought of her.

Kim excelled as an athlete during high school and college, whether she was playing basketball, volleyball, or softball. After graduating, Kim taught in an English-speaking school in Portugal for missionary children. From there she went on to teach in other Christian schools in Sao Paolo, Brazil; Ferguson, Missouri; and Seattle, Washington.

In December 2000, Kim and I married. She birthed and raised two incredible children: Joseph, now sixteen, and Jessa, fifteen. Throughout those years, Kim managed her roles as wife and mom while continuing her love for education and ministry. In 2009, she was named Teacher of the Year at Citrus Park Christian School in Tampa, Florida. Later she accepted a job to run an early education program at Atlantic Christian School, which earned a bronze medal in her second year as administrator. My wife has an incredible gift for loving people and bringing out their best.

After Superstorm Sandy hit the Northeast in October 2012, Kim started showing physical signs of muscle weakness. Unrelated to the storm, one of Kim's legs started to drag, causing her to fall several times. We knew something was wrong. Desperate to understand, we went to doctor after doctor after doctor before finally receiving a diagnosis in July 2015 of ALS (amyotrophic lateral sclerosis), better known as Lou Gehrig's disease. While thankful at last to have a diagnosis, we were devastated. There are no known causes or cures for this disease. The average life-span for a person with ALS is three to five years. Kim, now approaching her sixth year, continues to fight—and teach, parent, counsel, and write devotionals—all with her eyes.

Two years ago she received an eye-gaze computer that has now become her voice and only way to communicate. After calibrating the computer, Kim can text, send emails, surf the web, and write what God has placed on her heart just by moving her eyes. This book in your hands or on your screen is a compilation of what God has taught her beginning in February 2015 to January 2018.

During every stage of her life, Kim filled her time with ministry. She knows what it means to be set apart. This book of forty devotionals is no exception. God has allowed Kim's ministry to continue. As you read, I hope that Kim's struggles, pain, hurdles, and love for God will captivate you. She hopes you will be encouraged, challenged, and motivated so that you will see God and lean on him through your difficult times.

It's an honor to care for this beautiful woman of God. We pray that these devotionals will magnify and glorify our great God and Savior, Jesus Christ.

Louis Ordile

Everyone's in a Wheelchair

Written: February 2015

JEREMIAH 29:11–13

"For I know the plans I have for you," declares the LORD, "plans to prosper you and not to harm you, plans to give you hope and a future. Then you will call on me and come and pray to me, and I will listen to you. You will seek me and find me when you seek me with all your heart."

In 2012 my health started to decline. Today a wheelchair defines my reality. But God has graciously reminded me that everyone feels as though they are in a wheelchair: We all feel sometimes as though we've lost control. We find ourselves pushed in directions not originally planned. We fear going too fast or get frustrated by moving too slow. We experience the heartache of unfulfilled dreams, the anger that comes from limitations. We must cope with change that impacts identity, with anxiety and rejection, with pain, discontentment, and discomfort.

To resolve these feelings I must get on my knees before God. He's the only way. God loves me, and he loves you too. He longs to be in a relationship with us. Hard times cause our hearts to long for something deeper and real. We find what we are looking for when we are in a relationship with the God who created us.

Feelings handicap us all.

Accepting that Jesus is God's son and that he died and rose from the dead to pay for our sins is the only way to God. God is the only one that can give us peace, purpose, contentment, a true identity, and the security of being unconditionally loved.

> *For God so loved the world that he gave his one and only Son, that whoever believes in him shall not perish but have eternal life. (JOHN 3:16)*

I pray that no matter what your wheelchair looks like, what feelings may handicap you, that you will accept God's love for you. From where I sit, I have found his love true.

TODAY'S SONG
"I Will Rise" by Chris Tomlin

Master Mind

Written: January 9, 2016

PHILIPPIANS 2:13

… for it is God who works in you to will and to act in order to fulfill his good purpose.

$\mathcal{G}$rowing up I loved to play the game Mastermind. The premise of the game is to figure out the colors and the correct sequence of the four pegs that your opponent has selected at the start of the game. You must cipher the code by process of elimination within twelve attempts. Needless to say, this game requires ultimate levels of concentration and focus.

Every day I play a virtual game of Mastermind. God has assigned my role: I live with ALS. My version of the disease has disabled all my muscles from my mouth on down to my feet. The only thing I can control is my mind. Daily, I must choose what I will concentrate on. The Bible maps out a perfect strategy for me to win. The game is hard, but God has given me what I need to master my mind.

Do not be anxious about anything, but in every situation, by prayer and petition, with thanksgiving, present your requests to God. And the peace of God, which transcends all understanding, will guard your hearts and your minds in Christ Jesus. Finally, brothers and sisters, whatever is true, whatever is noble, whatever is right, whatever is pure, whatever is lovely, whatever is admirable—if anything is excellent or praiseworthy—think about such things. (PHIL. 4:6–8)

If anything is excellent or praiseworthy— think about such things.

I can only effectively think about one thing at a time. My prayer is that I will focus on how big God is and concentrate on his steadfast love. What is master of your mind?

TODAY'S SONG

"Perfect Peace" by Laura Story

7

Day 3

Daisy Day

Written: April 22, 2016

1 CORINTHIANS 13:4–8

Love is patient, love is kind. It does not envy, it does not boast, it is not proud. It does not dishonor others, it is not self-seeking, it is not easily angered, it keeps no record of wrongs. Love does not delight in evil but rejoices with the truth. It always protects, always trusts, always hopes, always perseveres. Love never fails.

We are taught to seek the appreciation, respect, approval, acceptance, and love of others. We fear being rejected, abandoned, abused, alone, and mocked if we don't seek approval. God did not design us to live this way; it leaves us with a broken heart.

God is the only one who can love me truly. Trying to make someone else love me will never satisfy the longing of my heart. God is the only one that will love me unconditionally. Nothing I do will make him love me more, and nothing I do will make him love me less.

God has, however, commanded me to love the people around me. 1 Corinthians 13 and Romans 12 tell me what it looks like to love. I am not to be kind so that you like me. I am to be kind because I love you, even if you don't love me in return. Ouch! So how can I do this?

"Will I love you?" and not "Will you love me?"

The first thing I must do, in order to love you, is get a daisy. Then, as I think of Jesus saving me from my sins by dying on the cross and rising again, I start pulling petals off, one by one. "He loves me, he loves me, he loves me..." Only when I am secure, confident, and full of God's love can I be brave enough to love you.

God never told me to live in a way that makes you love me. He just commanded me to love you. If our relationship is hard, then I need to ask the author of love to help me, not you. I can't love you the "1 Corinthians 13:4–8" way on my own. I need God's help.

So today, I might need a dozen daisies to remind myself of God's love for me before I can love you. Know that the challenge is not about you being difficult; it's about me learning to trust his love for me and obey.

TODAY'S SONG

"Beloved Let Us Love One Another" by Maranatha

Duct Tape

Written: May 12, 2016

PSALM 19:14

May these words of my mouth and this meditation of my heart be pleasing in your sight, Lord, my Rock and my Redeemer.

*I*f words could come out of my mouth, I would be deeply embarrassed by them. But, thankfully, my ALS is a built-in filter that protects the people around me from having to hear my unnecessary comments. I long to be spirit controlled without the Lord having to put duct tape on my mouth.

The book of James says that no one can tame the tongue. I know this is true. But I have been asking the Lord every morning to help me be a blessing. I want my words—the ones I can still communicate—to edify, not cause damage.

Being negative, critical, harsh, self-promoting, and putting others down only reveals a heart not yielded to the Lord. It shows that I, the one with a huge plank in my own eye, keep trying to point out the speck of dust in the eyes of others.

"Why do you look at the speck of sawdust in your brother's eye and pay no attention to the plank in your own eye? How can you say to your brother, 'Let me take the speck out of your eye,' when all the time there is a plank in your own eye? You hypocrite, first take the plank out of your own eye, and then you will see clearly to remove the speck from your brother's eye." (MATTHEW 7:3–5)

Be quick to listen, slow to speak.

I need spiritual duct tape. I need to take a moment to run the things I want to say before the Lord. To ask him to convict me before I make a mess. Only then can I encourage, affirm, defend, and speak the truth in love.

You would think being handicapped would make it easier not to sin. But I have more time to be still before the Lord—to see how much more I need to grow. Please pray for me. I long to be his voice when the spiritual duct tape comes off.

TODAY'S SONG
"Words" by Hawk Nelson

Day 5

Invictus

Written: May 13, 2016

2 CORINTHIANS 12:9–10

But he said to me, "My grace is sufficient for you, for my power is made perfect in weakness." Therefore I will boast all the more gladly about my weaknesses, so that Christ's power may rest on me. That is why, for Christ's sake, I delight in weaknesses, in insults, in hardships, in persecutions, in difficulties. For when I am weak, then I am strong.

Watching the Invictus Games, I wondered how some injured people can withstand great hardship and get back up when most cannot. What gives these athletes such extraordinary moxie?

During a vacation from college, I visited a church and found out that there would be a piano concert. What I didn't know is that the musician was blind. At the end of the service he turned to face the audience and stated his handicap. In spite of blindness he still had chosen to accomplish what God created him to do. He challenged me with the question, "What is your excuse?"

I had to think. What emotional handicap did I hide behind? What excuse did I use to avoid going outside my comfort zone? What did I miss out on because of fear? What would it take for me to get going on the grand avenue God has planned for me?

Invictus is Latin for "Unconquered."

The Invictus athletes didn't take the easy way out when tragedy hit; they figured out how to keep going. I don't know what drives them on an individual basis, but they all have an intense will to live. Today and for the rest of my life, I want to be an Invictus athlete in all that I encounter. I am not alone; the strength that I rely on comes from my big God. The best is yet to come.

TODAY'S SONG

"Worn" by Tenth Avenue North

Day 6

I'm Peculiar

Written: May 21, 2016

EPHESIANS 6:12–13

For our struggle is not against flesh and blood, but against the rulers, against the authorities, against the powers of this dark world and against the spiritual forces of evil in the heavenly realms. Therefore put on the full armor of God, so that when the day of evil comes, you may be able to stand your ground, and after you have done everything, to stand.

*S*ome might call me strange or odd; I say I am highly entertaining. ALS has caused me to drool often, to laugh and cry without control, to talk like a Wookie, to have a crooked smile, and to walk like the bride of Frankenstein. I'm unique even within the ALS community. And I praise the Lord for giving me the sense of humor to match my uniqueness.

I'm peculiar, however, in a much more important way. The word peculiar comes from the Latin word peculiaris meaning "private property, singular belonging to only one."

So I am peculiar because I belong to the Lord. I am his.

I'm peculiar in every sense of the word.

Every day I must choose to live in light of my position. I have an enemy that would love to devour me. He can't read my mind, but my posture, facial expressions, and tone reveal to him when I'm struggling. Being very competitive, I don't want to let Satan win. I have decided to follow Jesus. No turning back.

My heart breaks every time I read JOHN 6:67–69:

> *"You do not want to leave too, do you?" Jesus asked the Twelve. Simon Peter answered him, "Lord, to whom shall we go? You have the words of eternal life. We have come to believe and to know that you are the Holy One of God."*

Peter knew who Jesus was, and he wanted to stay with him. When things are tough, God asks me, "Will you leave me too?" I know who he is. There can be no turning back. I'm truly peculiar. I belong to the Lord. As long as I live, I am his.

TODAY'S SONG

"Whom Shall I Fear" by Chris Tomlin

Day 7

No Regrets

Written: May 23, 2016

MATTHEW 18:21–22

Then Peter came to Jesus and asked, "Lord, how many times shall I forgive my brother or sister who sins against me? Up to seven times?"

Jesus answered, "I tell you, not seven times, but seventy-seven times."

When my son was young he went through a phase of refusing to respond when someone in our family would give him a hug or tell him they loved him. Being concerned, I tried to communicate to him the importance of living with no regrets. I told him that I never wanted to leave things unsaid or unresolved because something might happen so that I never get another chance. He amazed me by his tender reply; it showed me just how much he had grown.

If you watch my son today, especially with his daddy, you will see love on display. Even more so now that I am sick, Joe has a big space in his heart for his daddy and family. But something even more evident has convicted and humbled me. Joe has an incredible ability to forgive.

I have observed several actions my son takes when he chooses to be at peace with someone. He grabs hold of understanding. He puts himself in their shoes to see their side. He shows compassion by considering what they are going through. He is willing to change himself to avoid being unnecessarily at odds with people.

Live as a merciful servant.

As an intense person with strong feelings, I need to get past myself and not make each situation all about me. Today I have a choice to forgive and be at peace. I want to forgive just like Joe. No regrets.

TODAY'S SONG
"Hello, My Name Is" by Mathew West

Day 8

Vulnerable

Written: May 25, 2016

2 PETER 1:3

His divine power has given us everything we need for a godly life through our knowledge of him who called us by his own glory and goodness.

$\mathscr{J}$esus asked the blind man, "What do you want me to do for you?"

My first thought about this question in Mark 10:51 was, "Duh, he wants to see." But did Jesus ask him sarcastically? No. He knew that the gift of sight would come at a price. If he healed him, Bartimaeus' life would change. He would have to learn to live as a healthy man who could see. That's why Jesus asked him what he wanted.

I thought this story was great until one day years back, at a time before I married, when Jesus asked me the same question. This time I said, "I don't want to be afraid. I don't want to let my fear of being abandoned dictate my relationships. I want to be healthy."

What would it look like, in this context, to live healthy? First, acknowledging that the Lord will never abandon me. Second, allowing myself to care about others and not running away if they

It's time to let you see me. All of me.

got to close. And lastly, I would permit myself to be vulnerable. I would give others the gift of sight into my true, inner self.

God knew the best partner for me. Someone who inspires me to do the right thing, who brings me flowers when I mess up, and who does not make fun of my quirks. Someone who supports my dreams, encourages me to step outside my comfort zone, and who demonstrates God's love to me at my most vulnerable times.

If I had not allowed God to heal my heart, I would never have married my husband. He continues to stand by me with my ALS. He won't allow me to return to my insecure ways. When I feel overwhelmed, embarrassed, dumb, shy, weak, or inadequate, he comes alongside me and literally helps me keep going.

I am vulnerable every moment of every day now, and I am not afraid. I have a big God who will never leave me and a husband who loves me by the grace of God. I am blessed.

TODAY'S SONG

"In the Eyes" by 1 Girl Nation

Day 9

Patience

Written: June 2, 2016

1 THESSALONIANS 5:14

And we urge you, brothers and sisters, warn those who are idle and disruptive, encourage the disheartened, help the weak, be patient with everyone.

*P*atience, a fruit of the Spirit, has never been a natural gift for me. First Thessalonians 5:14 hits me between the eyes because it lists the very character traits and failings that usually set me off. It ends with "be patient with everyone." Ironically, God not only has given me opportunities to practice patience throughout the years, but he has recently blessed me with an incredible role model.

Back in October, my sister-in-law Paula moved to our area to care for me when my family was not at home. She washed my hair and painted my toenails and everything in between. How she cared for me displayed a patience that goes beyond refusing to grow angry.

Patience is far more than avoiding huffiness, ignoring the time, or discounting how many times you have to repeat the same thing over and over. Someone with a lack of patience rolls their eyes, slams things, glares, and says hurtful words. Patience, as I have seen and experienced, is "doing." Patience displayed in a beautiful way leads to tenderness, helping when needed, making mundane tasks as pleasant as possible, not taking a quick offense, having a great sense of humor, going at the pace comfortable for the other person, having realistic expectations, and protecting someone from being embarrassed.

Patience accepts delay, trouble, or suffering without anger.

When we are truly gracious with each other, we find patience. This fruit of the Spirit is meant to be given freely to others. Everyone has the capability to demonstrate patience to someone else. I want to exhibit to others the patience that Paula has shown me. Pray for me as I ask God to help me be a blessing to others in the same way that I have been blessed. Fruity in a good way.

TODAY'S SONG

"Willing to Wait with Patience" by Veggie Tales

Trust Me

Written: June 6, 2016

ACTS 17:26–27

From one man he made all the nations, that they should inhabit the whole earth; and he marked out their appointed times in history and the boundaries of their lands. God did this so that they would seek him and perhaps reach out for him and find him, though he is not far from any one of us.

I was taken back by the movie Aladdin. My heart stopped when Aladdin reach out his hand to Jasmine from the magic carpet and dared her by saying, "Trust me." That is exactly what I want God to do for me. I want him to look me in the eyes, take me by the hand and say, "Come with me." I know that if he would ask me like that, I would gladly go.

God seems to like it best when he takes me on grand adventures alone, just the two of us. He knows that as long as I can depend on my friends and family around me, I will share less with him. He wants me to trust him and enjoy him.

The ALS journey the Lord has taken me on is rather unique. The only way I can communicate with anyone is with my eye-gaze computer. Dialogues are not really timely or elaborate. If you see me out in public, I observe silently and enjoy what

God has planned your every day. Go with him.

is going on around me. For the last two years I have learned to talk to the Lord directly from my heart. He not only understands what I am saying, but he knows how I feel. He understands and identifies with me. I am not lonely because the best Counselor is with me twenty-four hours a day. And he holds my hand.

Pray for me as I daily let the Lord look me in the eyes, take me by the hand, and ask me to trust him. I know that I don't want to miss out on all he has planned for me. He has planned every moment of my day for me to share with him. I get to explain, in detail, with the Lord the ups, downs and even the loops that make me sick to my stomach. He understands and holds my hand and smiles. This is what he always wanted.

TODAY'S SONG

"Take My Hand and Walk" by The Kry

B.E.S.T.

Written: June 9, 2016

PHILIPPIANS 1:9–11

*And this is my prayer: that your love may abound more and more
in knowledge and depth of insight, so that you may be able to
discern what is best and may be pure and blameless for the day
of Christ, filled with the fruit of righteousness that comes through
Jesus Christ—to the glory and praise of God.*

*E*very day I find that life should be evaluated by two
questions:

1. Am I giving my best effort?
2. Is this the best thing for me to do?

Everything I do has an impact on someone. Failure to give
my best in any situation will hurt not only me but also the people
I care about. Standing tall with a backbone of integrity does not
mean that I need to be perfect but for me to give my best effort.

The Bible is full of ordinary people who gave their best in
the best way when God asked it of them. We know and love
their stories because God always showed up on their behalf in

a big way. They were not perfect people, but they stood tall and allowed God to be seen: Daniel in the lion's den, Joshua at the walls of Jericho, and Queen Esther before the king.

Brave Enough to Stand Tall

Our world will not applaud a life sold out to the Lord. We often ask how much we can get away with, not what would be our best. If I live true to what God asks of me, I might be alone. But I will be in a great position to see God show up and do big things. It's never easy to tell the truth or avoid joining in on worldly fun. But our heroes of the Bible endured rejection, shared the gospel, were accused falsely, lived with convictions, confronted sin, and actively did what God asked of them when they faced intense opposition. They understood the cost.

I have choices to make every moment of every day. I am not working my way to heaven, or trying to get God to give me something, like an award or a pat on the back, or trying to look good in front of you. I want to live out my love for the Lord. He deserves my best effort and for me to do what is best: to be Brave Enough To Stand Tall for his glory. Do you give him your best?

TODAY'S SONG

"Whatever You Ask" by Steve Camp

Day 12

Advertising and Marketing

Written: June 14, 2016

PSALM 23:4–6

Even though I walk through the darkest valley, I will fear no evil, for you are with me; your rod and your staff, they comfort me. You prepare a table before me in the presence of my enemies. You anoint my head with oil; my cup overflows. Surely your goodness and love will follow me all the days of my life, and I will dwell in the house of the Lord forever.

I have often wondered how I would have responded if I had been one of the twelve disciples. As I read about their journey with Jesus, I find myself cringing. Jesus cared nothing about being politically correct, permissive, traditional, or making people comfortable. He spoke about the truth of the gospel and the Kingdom.

When I was in elementary school, my family attended Temple Baptist Church in Tacoma, Washington. Pastor Wagner closed the service one time by asking the Lord for the people to be miserable until they got right with God. I was shocked.

I peeked around to see if anyone else was surprised. That was the first time I heard anyone pray that way. I thought we were supposed to pray for people's happiness, health and comfy-ness.

How do you see God's power?

As a child, I prayed for everyone to get everything they wanted. Wouldn't that be the best way to attract people to the Lord? If I had been a disciple, I would have been the one asking Jesus if he really had to be so radical and extreme in his delivery. As you can tell, God didn't put me in charge of advertising and marketing. God does not need me to sell him or present Christianity in a clever or inviting way. God alone knows what it takes to draw people to him.

Today I sit before you in a wheelchair with ALS. After hundreds of prayers on my behalf, I have now asked the Lord again if ALS is the best way to advertise and market how powerful he is. As always, he just graciously reminds me that the marketing of God is his job. He knows what he wants to do in the hearts of the people I love.

You may dislike that I'm not praying for us to be happy, healthy, or comfy. I am, however, praying that we are right with God. A priceless prayer.

TODAY'S SONG

"Trust His Heart" by Babbie Mason

Day 13

Loud and Clear

Written: June 16, 2016

DEUTERONOMY 6:7

Impress them on your children. Talk about them when you sit at home and when you walk along the road, when you lie down and when you get up.

Through his kindness, God gave me a dad that spoke to me in a way I could understand and remember. My dad kept his words basic when it came to love, life, and living for Jesus. But how he lived showed me what he was saying, loud and clear.

Every single word of instruction my dad spoke to me, he demonstrated either before or after the fact, such as:

People who are hardest to love need love the most.

You are unique. Don't try to be like everyone else.

Don't seek revenge.

Pray about everything.

Concentrate on pleasing the Lord.

Have a grateful heart.

When you pray, expect God to answer.

Have a plan but leave room for the Lord to change it.

God is bigger than my enemy.

Don't quit because something is hard.

Be generous and willing to sacrifice for others.

Spend daily time reading the Bible and praying.

Give big hugs.

Give even bigger smiles.

Actions speak louder than words.

The Lord knew that I would learn best by observing. He gave me the opportunity to grow up being loved and coached by the best dad for me. Thank you, Dad, for all the truths you impressed on my heart. Your actions spoke louder than words. I heard you loud and clear. Love you.

TODAY'S SONG

"Find Us Faithful" by Steve Green

Day 14

Blessings

Written: July 4, 2016

PROVERBS 16:9
*In their hearts humans plan their course,
but the Lord establishes their steps.*

*E*ight years ago, my husband and I planned to leave the
Christian education ministry and become house par-
ents for a children's home in South Carolina. We desired to
be closer to my parents and to minister together as a family.
Excited about the possibility, we waited for our home to sell.
It didn't.

Where am I today? I live in South Carolina only thirty
minutes away from my parents. Ironically, because of ALS, we
later moved to where we wanted to be. My children get to be by
their grandparents for the first time. My husband doesn't have
to work full time and is able to spend more moments with me.
We have a beautiful place that is wheelchair friendly, and we can
minister as a family as God gives us opportunities. God wasn't
being mean by having us wait eight years; he just knew what

was coming. God knew that the best route to South Carolina was via New Jersey. He had divine appointments for us there with people who would impact, inspire, influence, teach, coach, mentor, disciple, love and demonstrate compassion. All part of his plan.

Hard times are God's mercies in disguise.

ALS can be a blessing only when God is the one in control. At the beginning of my ALS adventure, two dear New Jersey friends shared with me a song by Laura Story called "Blessings." Even though I cannot speak, a week doesn't go by that I don't sing that song in my heart. It reminds me that the hard times are God's mercies in disguise. He alone knows how to work all things out for good. I am learning to trust that God will ultimately answer my prayers in a perfect way in his time.

TODAY'S SONG

"Blessings" by Laura Story

A New Way to Count to Ten

Written: July 6, 2016

PSALM 94:18–19
When I said, "My foot is slipping,"
your unfailing love, LORD, supported me.
When anxiety was great within me,
your consolation brought me joy.

have always struggled with a temper. I would do my best to anticipate potential obstacles in order to prepare myself mentally. Sadly, this method does not always prevent me from getting mad. More recently, God has given me a new approach.

During our move from New Jersey to South Carolina, I found myself having to deal with my anger in a new way. As I sat in my wheelchair, unable to communicate effectively and unable to help physically, I grew mad. I wanted to be involved, have things completed in certain ways, and help with all that had to be done. But I couldn't. The ironic twist to my temper is that I can no longer mask it or hide it. Anger causes my muscles to seize up, and I can't move. Comically, for those observing this grand display of immaturity, I then get even more irate that I got mad in the first place. At this point, I am completely paralyzed. I end up in my bedroom, bent over in my

Thy will be done (1), thy will be done (2), thy will be done (3)...

wheelchair, trying to breathe, waiting for my muscles to relax.

In one of these moments, God brought to mind the song "Thy Will" by Hillary Scott. Instead of counting to ten, I sing "Thy Will Be Done" ten times. In the process of saying these four words I am reminded that God is in control. He has a plan, no one can stop him, and I am secure in his hands. This is my new way of dealing with my anger: "Thy Will Be Done" ten times. You will probably still see me get angry, but please pray that I surrender my will to his and sing "Thy Will Be Done."

Oh, and for the record, God sent an army of people to help pack, clean, load, drive, unload, and unpack. He provided abundantly, perfectly suited to his plan. His will was better than my plans.

TODAY'S SONG

"Thy Will" by Hillary Scott and the Scott Family

Honor

Written: July 10, 2016

ROMANS 12:9–10

Love must be sincere. Hate what is evil; cling to what is good. Be devoted to one another in love. Honor one another above yourselves.

In college, I called my mom to complain about a professor. Several girls had left the class in tears after the first round of presentations. Why did the teacher have to be so harsh? How rude! What Mom said next changed everything.

She proceeded to tell me to go to class early and try to get to know the professor. I was stunned. Where was the pity and compassion I expected to receive? Why didn't my mom feel sorry for me and tell me to drop the class? I hung up the phone trying to figure out what had just happened.

Deep inside I knew Mom was right. But would the professor really respond any differently one-on-one? Monday night came, and I made my way to class thirty minutes early. The professor sat at her desk, dressed in her power suit with a frowny face. I laid out my materials and pretended to work. I dared to break the silence. I simply asked, "How's your day?" By the time class started, I felt like crying. Not for me but for my professor.

Honor: to regard with great respect.

After teaching at a local Christian school in the daytime, she would go directly to the hospital to visit her mom who was dying of cancer. Then she would come to teach us at night.

As the girls filed in, I knew they had bitterness in their hearts toward her. I also knew that she had nothing left to give by the time she got to us. After class I went to all the girls to let them know that we could make a difference. We all decided to be loving and compassionate by giving smiles and compliments and not being quick to take offense.

It's easy to gossip, repay a snub with a snub, give minimal effort, and ignore those around us. But my mom taught me how to respond to people with honor. She has spent countless hours on the phone listening, has opened her home for strangers, has delivered homemade gourmet meals, and has kept secrets in confidence. No matter what, my mom treats people with honor and respect.

Even though I wanted my mom to feel sorry for me so many years ago, learning this lesson was far more valuable. By her example of love and compassion, I understand what honor looks like.

TODAY'S SONG
"Others" by Israel Houghton

All Things to All People

Written: August 2, 2016

1 CORINTHIANS 9: 22–23

To the weak I became weak, to win the weak. I have become all things to all people so that by all possible means I might save some. I do all this for the sake of the gospel, that I may share in its blessings.

*T*oday my husband took our children, Joe and Jessa, to register for school. Besides being new to the area, they will attend their first year in public school. I am nervous for them. They will be exposed to new things that will define them spiritually, emotionally, and academically. I have so many things that I want to tell them; however, God brings me back to 1 Corinthians 9:19–23.

In this passage of scripture, the Apostle Paul keeps the goal and method simple to understand: be a servant of others to the point of becoming all things to all people in order to win them to Christ. Simple to understand but hard to live.

Paul understood the concept attributed to Theodore Roosevelt: "People don't care how much you know until they know how much you care." Paul knew that the gateway to sharing Jesus with someone is first to identify with them and understand what they are going through. He did not compromise his relationship with the Lord, but he focused on serving others in a way to give them hope. He knew the value of walking in their shoes. He didn't waste time judging but tried to figure out how to win them to Christ. Everyone has needs, and he wasn't shocked by how others lived.

Figure out how you can win others to Christ.

Joe and Jessa, when you go to school today, you will see all kinds of people. They all need Jesus and they all have hurts. Your mission, should you choose to accept it, is to become all things to all people to win them to Christ. Some will be difficult to figure out because they hide behind the way they dress, their anger, laughter, accomplishments, fear, money, poverty, disabilities and more. Take time to understand the people God puts in your path. Pray for wisdom to see them the way God sees them and for strength to serve them in order to share Jesus and give them hope. There has been no greater moment to live for the Lord.

TODAY'S SONG
"Be the One" by Al Denson

Schooled by Junior Highers

Written: August 5, 2016

JAMES 5:16

Therefore confess your sins to each other and pray for each other so that you may be healed. The prayer of a righteous person is powerful and effective.

When I taught junior high I wanted the classroom to be a safe place. I wouldn't allow my students to be mean to each other. This also included how I treated and respected them. A great plan, in theory.

One afternoon we sat in a circle playing an interactive review game, having fun—until someone gave the wrong answer. Immediately, a young lady began to laugh and mock the student who messed up. I quickly spoke up, and she stopped talking. But I didn't. In front of everyone, I proceeded to tell her how wrong she was. With each passing moment, her shoulders slumped lower and lower. By the time I finished, no one was speaking or smiling

Later that evening, the Holy Spirit spoke to me, "So how was your day? Is there anything you should have done differently?" I evaluated the events from earlier and winced at the review game debacle. I had stopped the young lady from mocking, but in the process I had mocked her. She expected certain correction from me, but by her body language now etched in my mind, I realized I had done damage. Now the fun part—apologizing.

They held me to a high standard and challenged me.

The next morning as I walked across the playground, guess who was the first person to come and give me a hug? The thought that everything was cool and I wouldn't need to say anything crossed my mind. I dismissed that fleeing thought, however, and said to her in private, "Laughing at someone when they make a mistake is wrong, but how I handled the situation was also wrong. I'm so sorry. Please forgive me."

"Sure, Miss Kenyon, I knew you were going to say that," she replied.

Junior high students are quick to forgive. I discovered that to be true on more than one occasion. God used them to teach me not to be afraid to admit my sin. In return I experienced love and understanding. They held me to a high standard and challenged me. God knew that I needed them in my life to demonstrate how I need to respond to others and to be real.

TODAY'S SONG

"1 Timothy 4:12" by Seeds Family Worship

Spaghetti and Meatballs

Written: August 16, 2016

ISAIAH 40:30–31

Even youths grow tired and weary,
and young men stumble and fall;
but those who hope in the Lord
will renew their strength.
They will soar on wings like eagles;
they will run and not grow weary,
they will walk and not be faint.

The verb "wait" makes me laugh. A verb denotes action. If I truly wait, I don't move or act. Honestly, this rarely happens. I end up fidgeting, complaining, coming up with another idea, giving up, settling for something less, moving on, getting discouraged, or becoming fearful or even angry.

Isaiah 40:30–31 stumped me until I heard my husband say that he was making spaghetti and meatballs. Last Friday, Lou invited my parents to come over Sunday, after church, for his famous Italian dinner. Instantly my mouth started to water. It was only Friday. I would have to wait, gladly.

I was not just waiting on spaghetti and meatballs. I was waiting on Lou to make his spaghetti and meatballs. I was excited and eager. I watched. I anticipated. And I had no thoughts about trying to help him. I was exceedingly confident in what he was going to do. For the first time, I understood Isaiah 40:30–31.

When Lou makes meatballs, they are epic.

When I wait on the Lord, I am renewed and strengthened. I can also run and soar. The key is the one on whom I am waiting. Spaghetti and meatballs are good, but when Lou makes them, they are epic. I know because I know Lou. Whatever he makes, I know I will love it. Likewise, when I wait on the Lord, my focus needs to be on who he is. Then I will be excited to wait for what he is going to do. God wants me to wait on him like I wait for Lou's spaghetti and meatballs.

TODAY'S SONG

"How Great Is Our God" by Chris Tomlin

Day 20

Mistakes

Written: August 22, 2016

LUKE 7:47

"Therefore, I tell you, her many sins have been forgiven—as her great love has shown. But whoever has been forgiven little loves little."

This morning I prayed for Joe and Jessa as they walked out the door for school. I prayed that they would be a light and grow in their love for the Lord. When I finished praying, my thoughts went to Luke 7, a story about a prostitute who responded to Jesus with extravagant love because she had been forgiven much. To drive home this incredible story, Jesus told those in the house a parable about two men who owed debts to the same moneylender. One owed a tremendous amount more than the other, but both were pardoned. Then Jesus asked, "Which one will love the moneylender more?"

If I ask the Lord to increase the love that Joe and Jessa have for him, then they have to understand of how much they have been forgiven. They are not just forgiven for the sins that they have already committed, but those that they will commit in the future. That means that they will make mistakes, do wrong things, and intentionally sin. As their mom, I don't like this method. But I know that it is what's best for them in their walk with the Lord. The more they fail, the more op-

Forgive Much = Love Much

portunities they'll have to grow in their love for the Lord.

I heard a D.A.R.E. instructor say to my students in Florida, "You are going to make mistakes. That's how you learn." So when—not if—my children make a mistake, I want to use that moment to share Luke 7 with them.

Paul enumerates a long list of sins in 2 Timothy 3:2–5. These alone as potential wrongs my children will commit are a hard pill to swallow:

> *People will be lovers of themselves, lovers of money, boastful, proud, abusive, disobedient to their parents, ungrateful, unholy, without love, unforgiving, slanderous, without self-control, brutal, not lovers of the good, treacherous, rash, conceited, lovers of pleasure rather than lovers of God— having a form of godliness but denying its power. Have nothing to do with such people.*

However, the more Joe and Jessa can learn to stand in front of the mirror of God's word, the more their love will grow for the one who paid to pardon them.

TODAY'S SONG

"Broken and Spilled Out" by Steve Green

43

I Can't Complain

Written: August 29, 2016

1 THESSALONIANS 5:16–18

Rejoice always; pray continually, give thanks in all circumstances; for this is God's will for you in Christ Jesus.

In John's gospel, after Peter had denied Jesus three times, Jesus asked Peter, "Simon son of John do you love me more than these? ... Simon son of John, do you [truly] love me? ... Simon son of John, do you love me?" (21:15–17). In those three questions, Jesus offered Peter restoration by allowing him to change each of his three denials into affirmations of love.

As soon as Peter confirmed his devotion, he again felt the danger of identifying himself as Jesus's loyal follower. Jesus followed his questions with an explanation of how Peter would die. Peter immediately looked around, pointed in John's direction, and asked, "What about him?" Jesus then said to him, "What is that to you? You follow me" (21–22).

I can't imagine how Jesus must have felt. He had just gone through the most horrific death, experienced excruciating physical and emotional pain, and endured brutal humiliation. Now he speaks to the most headstrong and gregarious disciple about his devotion to him. When Jesus implied the kind of death Peter would have to die, Peter complains. "What about him?" Why didn't Peter respond

What is that to you?

with, "That's nothing compared to what you just went through" or "When that time comes I won't deny you again" or "I want to obey the Father like just you did" or even better still, "I will bravely show the world that I love you. Thank you for investing in me and loving me."

It's so easy to judge Peter for being impulsive, faint of heart, and immature. However, years later when he was going to be crucified, he asked to be hung upside-down, feeling unworthy of the same death that Jesus suffered. Peter became the disciple that Jesus knew he could be.

When I complain of my ALS, I display no strength of character, spirit, control, allegiance, or gratitude. So to identify with Jesus, I mentally put myself at the foot of the cross and hear him say to me, "What is that to you? You follow me." Then my ALS seems like nothing in comparison to what Jesus has done.

TODAY'S SONG

"Turn Your Eyes upon Jesus" sung by Michael W. Smith

Fire Is Needed

Written: September 16, 2016

JAMES 1:2–4

*Consider it pure joy, my brothers and sisters, whenever you face
trials of many kinds, because you know that the testing of your
faith produces perseverance. Let perseverance finish its work so
that you may be mature and complete, not lacking anything.*

*N*o one enjoys stress, tragedies, or being under fire.
Most of us tend to quit, pull away emotionally, or
avoid conflict. But the Lord, in his divine wisdom, has given
a tremendous example of what fire can produce in us. The
Yosemite National Park holds a powerful illustration of
needed fire.

When this area was declared to be a National Park, the
park management began efficiently extinguishing its naturally
occurring fires. Over time, the number of new trees diminished.
Scientists finally realized that the Giant Sequoias in the Mariposa
Grove needed fire to reproduce. The heat triggers the cones of
the Giant Sequoias to birth seeds, and the fire clears out the

brush, making room for new growth. An amazing feature of the Giant Sequoia itself is that the fire does not seem to affect the tree. Even when every other tree around it goes up in flames, Sequoias remain unscathed

Fires refine us, purify us, and test us.

due to their virtually fireproof bark. God gave them extra thick bark to withstand this astonishing process and protect the heart of the tree.

The Giant Sequoias do what they were created to do. Their example is powerful. When the fire comes, they stand strong. They multiply through the flames. They stand as magnificent testaments to their Creator. The Giant Sequoias were created to glorify the Lord.

Like the Giant Sequoias, God puts us through fires we call "trials." Trials test us, refine us, purify us, and rid us of the brush in our lives so that we can be and do what God created us to be and do. He also promises to walk with us through these fires, as he did with Shadrach, Meshach, and Abednego (Dan. 3:19–27). No one would willingly walk into a fire. But if Jesus reached out from that fire to take our hands to lead us to the other side, then might we be willing to go? Remember, God created us to glorify and enjoy him forever.

TODAY'S SONG

"Go Out with Joy" by The Maranatha Singers

Behind Door Number One

Written: October 11, 2016

ROMANS 8:28

*And we know that in all things God works for the good of those
who love him, who have been called according to his purpose.*

$\mathcal{I}$ first started having ALS symptoms in October of 2012,
but not until August of 2015 did we receive a diagnosis.
During those four years, determined to find out what was
going on, my husband took me to fifteen different medical
professionals. It made me feel like a contestant on the TV
game show, *Let's Make a Deal*. What's behind Door Number
One, Door Number Two, and Door Number Three?

As a child I loved the suspense of not knowing. The not
knowing made the show exciting. After all, I wasn't the contestant—so it didn't really matter to me whether the door revealed
a good or bad prize. I just wanted to know. Now, I considered
each doctor's door a possible answer to my health questions.
Now I was the contestant and the game affected me from head
to toe. And it was scary.

When we finally opened the last door, Door Number One,
we officially knew the disease that plagued me. I didn't cry,
throw up, or scream, though I may have done all of those things
back in 2012 if someone had told me I had ALS. When we left

Robert Woods Johnson Hospital at Rutgers, I told Lou we should go out for ice cream because peace filled my heart. Through the process of not knowing, the Lord had been preparing me. He kept reminding me that he knew

Are you prepared to see behind Door Number One?

what was wrong. He could see behind and beyond any doors in my life. We would find out what was wrong when God thought it best.

When Door Number One finally opened, I was ready. Doors two, three, and many others had prepared me for the final reveal. Each previous door opened when test results came back: no MS, no Lyme disease, no brain tumor, no Gillian Barre, no brain bacteria, no cancer, no toxins in my blood, no infectious diseases, no spinal cord lesions, and no digestive system complications.

Any of these other "wonderful" possibilities that I had been tested for were formidable issues. God knew the best way to get me mentally prepared. He got me to be thankful for what I did not have. Ironically, the same trick still works. I am still able to be thankful for ALS and that I don't have a list of other deadly diseases. I am thankful for Door Number One and I am counting my blessings.

TODAY'S SONG

"Accentuate the Positive" by Bing Crosby

49

Figure It Out

Written: September 24, 2016

PHILIPPIANS 4:13

I can do all this through him who gives me strength.

*I*n high school and college, I spent my summers working construction with a man named Corky Hogaboam,
whom I called "Sir." Because he was an incredible teacher
and mentor, he taught me everything about flooring, painting, and roofing. One day while prepping the outside of a
home to paint, I tried to get a light fixture off the side of a
house. I had a bear of a time and thought they must have
built the house around this light. I found Sir and told him
that I couldn't get the fixture down. Without frustration or
anger, he told me it didn't matter how much time it took,
only that I needed to figure it out. Ten minutes later I came
back to report my victory.

When I lost the ability to grip things with my hands, Debbie
Smallwood, my speech therapist, taught me how to successfully
drink water out of a martini glass by tilting the glass without

having to pick it up. Genius. That is, until last month. Three days in a row I ended up choking and gagging. I couldn't drink. Awake in bed, I asked the Lord to help me. With his assistance I realized that in the process of trying to hang

Are you determined, or do you give up?

on to the glass with my mouth, I had pulled myself too close to the table. My neck bent to far forward, which prevented me from swallowing freely. The next day I sat at a different angle to drink. No problems.

The Bible tells me that when I need wisdom, I can always pray and ask God who gives generously to all. He is the one I can go to when I can't do what is being asked of me. His goal is not to make my life easy but that I should be determined to figure it out. He knows that with every hurdled obstacle my faith will grow. I will learn that all things are possible.

TODAY'S SONG

"You Are My Strength" by Hillsong Untied

Life Support

Written: November 20, 2016

1 PETER 5:6–7

Humble yourselves, therefore, under God's mighty hand, that he may lift you up in due time. Cast all your anxiety on him because he cares for you.

This last week I received my breathing apparatus. With ALS, the final culprit that usually steals life is respiratory-related. My new, proactive doctor prescribed the equipment needed on my initial visit. When he described the different machines, he called one "the Trilogy." He explained that the name didn't have anything to do with spiritual things, only its function. The therapist who works with the machines at our home refers to them as "Life Support."

The equipment that they gave me hasn't immediately improved the quality of my life. Quite the contrary. The Trilogy has proven to need acquired skills. With hours of practice, I may be able to figure out how to benefit from the breath that it is designed to give me. But right now, even though the therapist keeps telling me that over time my body will sync with the Trilogy and that I should even be able to use it to sleep better at night, my muscles want to lock up and fight against the flow of air being pumped in and out of the mask.

Where does your breath come from?

Whether I ever figure out this breathing machine, I have been given true Life Support—the Lord, who ultimately determines my days. I will have breath as long as God provides. Similarly, when I am not in sync with the Lord, I end up fighting what he designed for my good. I must learn to yield to him in every situation to benefit from all that God has for me. I should even be able to sleep peacefully at night.

To be honest with you, the thought of suffocating is my all-time worst fear. I don't think that this is a coincidence. Learning to live each moment without being in fear of dying requires that I learn to trust my Life Support, physically and spiritually. If I practice and concentrate trying to be in sync with my machine and the Lord, I will have more confidence. Trilogy. Trinity. Life Support. Just breathe.

TODAY'S SONG
"Breathe" by Jonny Diaz

Falling Down

Written: November 28, 2016

PSALM 34:19–20

The righteous person may have many troubles,
but the Lord delivers him from them all;
he protects all his bones,
not one of them will be broken.

*S*everal years ago, before my diagnosis with ALS, I fell flat thirty times. I have done it all: landed on my knees, on my hands, on my butt, my elbows, my face, my ear, and on the back of my head. I fell on the sidewalk, the street, the boardwalk, at work, at home, at the doctor's office, and at a restaurant. I kept saying, "I can overcome what's wrong with my muscles." Then I finally got smart enough and started using a wheelchair.

In all my tumbles I never broke a bone or had a concussion. The Lord had appointed some swift and strong guardian angels to take care of me. I would scold them when I would fall, but I also always realized that it could have been much worse.

These falls often made me think about Job. God permitted Satan to mess with Job, but God set the parameters. How could I have fallen that many times, unable to catch myself with my hands, and not break anything? With each fall

Help, I've fallen and I can't get up.

God reminded me that I was part of a bigger plan and he has set the parameters. As I applied ice to my boo-boos, a peace would rush over me. I experienced God's protection in a powerful way. The miracle was not in the fall, but in how I was held when I did fall. Being broken was not part of the arrangement; being protected was and still is.

I hate to fall. My heart races, my skin burns, and my muscles ache. But being able to get back up is a huge blessing. I might be a little scratched and dented, but I'm not broken. I'm not broken in mind or in body. This morning when I read Psalm 34:19–20, it made me smile. No matter what happens to me I have confidence that God, not Satan, determines the boundaries around me. My heart and body are held in God's hands. No bubble wrap needed.

TODAY'S SONG

"Jesus Take the Wheel" by Carrie Underwood

Day 27

He Knows and Understands

Written: December 11, 2016

HEBREWS 4:14–16

*Therefore, since we have a great high priest who has ascended
into heaven, Jesus the Son of God, let us hold firmly to the faith
we profess. For we do not have a high priest who is unable to
empathize with our weaknesses, but we have one who has been
tempted in every way, just as we are—yet he did not sin. Let us
then approach God's throne of grace with confidence, so that we
may receive mercy and find grace to help us in our time of need.*

When I was a child, Christmas taught me that Jesus
was the best gift ever. As I headed to college,
Christmas illustrated that Jesus came to rescue me. As I
became a mommy, Christmas gripped my heart with the sor-
row for the sacrifice of a loved child for someone else's sake.
Today, now that I have ALS, Christmas demonstrates to me
the extent Jesus was willing to go to identify with me.

Jesus came to earth, fully God and fully man. But he didn't
teleport. He didn't start as a man. He came as a baby. Jesus had

to depend on others to feed him, change his diapers, dress him, bathe him, wipe his nose, carry him, and protect him. He gave up his power, his control, and his crown to be

Jesus identifies with me.

humiliated. Jesus willingly came as a baby so that he could identify with me, and so I could learn how to depend on others. If the Creator could fulfill God's purpose when Jesus was a baby, so can I.

Jesus understands me. He endured everything for my benefit. I'm not the first one to be humbled and I won't be the last. He came to show me how to live in obedience to God, to have no temper tantrums. Keeping the mental picture of baby Jesus in my mind encourages my heart. If he could do it, so can I with his help. I can be a big baby.

TODAY'S SONG

"He Knows" by Jeremy Camp

Word of the Year

Written: January 8, 2017

ROMANS 5:1–2

Therefore, since we have been justified through faith, we have
peace with God through our Lord Jesus Christ, through whom
we have gained access by faith into this grace in which we now
stand. And we boast in the hope of the glory of God.

*M*y friend Mindy picks one word to focus on each year. After much thought, I chose "faith" to be my word for this year. I chose faith initially because the word would remind me to focus on Jesus, the object of my faith. But later I came to realize that God put faith on my heart because he knows that I still have much to learn and understand.

I have been wondering what to do with the verses in James that tell me that faith without works is dead. I have ALS and no active ministry role. I am no longer able to volunteer in the nursery or teach Sunday School or go on mission trips. I'm unable to make meals for families in the church or community. I can't speak to share the gospel of Jesus or to sing worship songs. I can't extend my arms to give hugs, take a pen to write encouraging notes, or even grab hold of someone's hand to pray with them. What good works can I do to demonstrate my faith?

Do your works demonstrate your faith?

This year I discovered that I'm asking the wrong question. The question should be, "What works is God doing in and through me?" The works that accompany my faith show God's work in me. As God works in me, it will result in me acting out. I will end up doing the most unnatural, uncomfortable, unexpected, unseen, unsafe, unprofitable, and unselfish work. My faith will ultimately result in works that could only be done by God. I am thankful that my wheelchair can't get in God's way.

TODAY'S SONG

"Look Me in the Heart" by Wayne Watson

HGTV and Me

Written: March 6, 2017

PSALM 138:8
The Lord will vindicate me;
your love, Lord, endures forever—
do not abandon the works of your hands.

I have been brought to tears trying to use my electric wheelchair in our cozy home. This gift of power and mobility has not made things easier, just more humiliating. Trying to hold my hand steady and make smooth adjustments with the joystick has actually been quite scary. I could star in my own HGTV comedy series called *Hit* about high-speed room redesign.

I received the electric wheelchair because of my limitations. The only requirement was that I finally had to admit that I needed it. The irony was that in the process of trying to use what was designed to help me, I made my disabilities more glaring. I can no longer hide the reality of my condition. When I come into a room, you know right away that I have a physical handicap.

The process of learning to use the electric wheelchair reminds me to let God move me. Becoming a child of God required me to admit my sin and my need to be rescued. Even though I

Now the whole world knows.

have the power that raised Jesus from the dead at my disposal, I still have to learn to live in that freedom. I am not saved so that you don't see my sin. I am saved so that regardless of my sin, God will do what is necessary to make me more like Jesus. I like the sound of that. It reminds me of another HGTV show, this one an old favorite: *Divine Design*.

TODAY'S SONG

"I Will Serve You" by Maranatha

Pass the Baton

Written: July 14, 2017

2 KINGS 2:9

When they had crossed, Elijah said to Elisha, "Tell me, what can I do for you before I am taken from you?"

When the doctor informed me that I had ALS, I pictured myself in a virtual line of people I loved, waiting for our imminent day with the Lord. God had chosen to call these people home with a timing that surprised me: Susan Finkbiener, my high school youth leader and role model; Jane Meacham, fellow teacher and my precious mentor; Howard Presnall, my prayer warrior partner; and, Megan Johnson, my former student who had an incredible testimony of God's grace. Why did God take them to heaven ahead of me?

Each one possessed talent, skill, charisma, boldness, courage, and influence—qualities that they used for God's glory. When God took them home, my heart hurt. Knowing that they had lived victoriously in spite of their obstacles inspired me. They praised the Lord and came to peace. God worked in and through them in a big way. Even now their legacy carried on.

In the relay of life, we receive encouragement from one another.

Elisha didn't want Elijah to go, either. But Elisha asked Elijah to allow him to have the same power that he had used in his ministry. Elisha wanted to be able to carry on the mission. So here I sit in my purple wheelchair wanting to do the same. In the relay of life, my dear teammates are no longer here. I'm not able to replace them or to fill their shoes, but I can continue to proclaim that the God they served is bigger than my obstacles. I will pick up the baton and, in their honor and for his glory, live yielded to his will as they did. He is worthy.

TODAY'S SONG

"These Walls" by Jason David

Sustained

Written: August 6, 2017

PSALM 126:2

Our mouths were filled with laughter,
our tongues with songs of joy.
Then it was said among the nations,
"The LORD has done great things for them."

For the past three years I have been routinely meeting
with ALS multidisciplinary teams. Several professionals
have come together to care for me and monitor my health.
They assess my breathing, reflexes, strength, coordination,
range of motion, blood pressure, weight, diet and nutrition,
and lab work. They focus on evaluating my decline to try to
prepare me for the worst. It is not my favorite. It exhausts
me emotionally, especially when we get home. But not this
last visit.

I asked a couple of people to pray with me that the team
would see that God alone sustains me. When Lou and I met with
the repository specialist, we giggled trying to get the mouthpiece

situated in my mouth. The test that examines muscle strength from head to toe showed no diminished strength within the

Prayer and Laughter: medicine that sustains.

prior three months. Everyone got excited about my diaphragm strength. Then my husband shared the good news of being given cases of organic food supplements designed for my feeding tube. I could not help but laugh because of the prayer.

Astonishingly, for the first time ever, the doctor didn't ask if we wanted medicine for my Bulbar Affect laughter. He just joined in with me. He acknowledged that my laughter came from my heart, not my spastic muscles.

God sustains me completely. He supplies peace, comfort, hope and support. No one can measure that impact on a scale, chart, or even by comparing me to others. The fact that Lou and I can sit in the doctor's office and laugh together is a gift that God has given us. Laughter is priceless when mingled with pain and suffering. Life is not easy for anyone. Only God can sustain us through it all.

TODAY'S SONG

"Cast Your Burdens upon Jesus" by He Cares For You

Awful to Awesome

Written: August 13, 2017

JAMES 1:16–17

Don't be deceived, my dear brothers and sisters. Every good and
perfect gift is from above, coming down from the Father of the
heavenly lights, who does not change like shifting shadows.

One Sunday four years ago, I sat in my lightweight transport wheelchair in the handicap section at Greentree Church in New Jersey. A male guest who had two caregivers sat in a huge electric wheelchair in the front row and completely distracted me because his chair was much, much bigger than mine. I wanted to avoid being in his position as long as possible. I felt sorry for him.

This last Thursday I had an incredible opportunity at an event that I had been looking forward to for months. Ironically, the reason for the excitement had to do with my now huge electric wheelchair and conversion van. My daughter Jessa played in her first volleyball match of the season. From the front-row seat, I watched in comfort and safety, supported by my chair. The rather conspicuous wheelchair gave me the ability to enjoy every minute of my daughter's four-game match. My mommy heart was ecstatic.

A dreaded existence becomes a place of sweet comfort.

The piece of medical equipment that I thought represented a dreaded existence now was my ticket to an amazing life. God in his grace has given me a wonderful family to enjoy and make memories with from my wheelchair. What I once viewed as awful is now awesome.

Four years ago, I missed a chance to celebrate that the guest who sat in his big chair in the front row had made it to church. If God can use what I now call an awesome electric wheelchair, nothing is too awful for him to transform.

TODAY'S SONG

"You Raise Me Up" by Josh Groban

Day 33

I Celebrate You

Written: August 22, 2017

1 PETER 3:7–8

*Husbands, in the same way be considerate as you live with your
wives, and treat them with respect as the weaker partner and
as heirs with you of the gracious gift of life, so that nothing will
hinder your prayers.*

*F*or the last week I have listened to sermons and studied
the Bible to learn more about marriage. I want to be a
better wife. Being handicapped means that I must go back to
the drawing board and figure out what I can do to accomplish what God asks of me. Daily, Lou loves and cares for me
as my primary care giver and the head of our household. I
have become convicted that God wants me to fully respect
Lou beyond my simply grateful heart.

In a dark hour, I saw Lou in a deeper way. In the middle of
the night I could not breathe. My body went into complete
panic-attack mode. I couldn't move or communicate. I lay there
completely helpless. Lou, caught completely off guard, woke up

and saved my life. His natural instincts went into motion; he knew exactly what to do. Afterwards, he proceeded to tend to me physically and emotionally for the rest of the night.

For in sickness and in health, till death do us part.

Later, my mind raced thinking of all that had happened. In the process of me praying, "God help me to be a better wife," my husband had come to my rescue. I'm convinced that God wants me to celebrate Lou rather than being merely thankful. I get to highlight the character of his heart. God has given me the privilege to honor Lou and to notice all that God is doing in and through him daily. Lou is living proof that a "1 Peter 3:7–8" man exists. Celebrate the husband God gave you with me.

TODAY'S SONG

"The Marriage Prayer" by John Waller

Symbiotic

Written: August 27, 2017

MATTHEW 28:19–20

*"Therefore go and make disciples of all nations, baptizing them in
the name of the Father and of the Son and of the Holy Spirit, and
teaching them to obey everything I have commanded you. And
surely I am with you always, to the very end of the age."*

*M*ost friendships form from commonalities, things
people have in common. As a science teacher,
though, I love symbiotic relationships: two unalike crea-
tures mutually benefitting each other. Often one of the crea-
tures could inflict harm on the other, but instead it chooses
to protect. This dynamic sometimes found in the animal
kingdom illustrates what God wants of humankind.

Several years ago my younger friend Traci, a Gen X'er, started
an OWLS ministry at First Baptist Church of Lexington. She
wanted to encourage the Older, Wiser, Loving, Seniors (OWLS).
In many ways, they relationship they created was symbiotic. Last
Thursday I attended a surprise birthday party for Traci, spon-

sored by her OWLS. The generational gap created no interference for their mutual admiration and care. When Traci came into the room, I cried, knowing they the OWLS had met a special need of hers.

Doting on Older, Wiser, Loving, Seniors

Oh, how our world needs to see Christians demonstrate care and respect! Our tendency to fight and attack people who are different benefits no one. Symbiotic behavior requires actively meeting a need and valuing what another person has to offer. Being different is not a barrier but simply an obstacle to overcome.

Jesus commissioned us to make disciples of all nations. We need to be in relationships for this to happen. Traci and the OWLS demonstrate what God wants of you and me.

TODAY'S SONG

"Love in Any Language" by Sandy Patty

Factory Reset

Written: December 1, 2017

HEBREWS 4:12–13

*For the word of God is alive and active. Sharper than any
double-edged sword, it penetrates even to dividing soul and spirit,
joints and marrow; it judges the thoughts and attitudes of the
heart. Nothing in all creation is hidden from God's sight. Everything is uncovered and laid bare before the eyes of him to whom
we must give account.*

I had significant issues with my eye-gaze computer last
month. My husband spent hours on the phone with
different representatives trying to solve the problem. We
unplugged, rebooted, uninstalled, downloaded, and updated,
but nothing worked. Even when the technicians took over
my computer via Wi-Fi, it continued to glitch. The same
malfunction alert popped up each time: "internal error."

We finally got to the point where their only remaining
suggestion was to do a factory reset. If that didn't correct the
problem, we would have to send the computer in to be repaired.

Sending it for repair meant a whole month without my computer. My eye-gaze computer is the only way I can communicate with my family, keep in touch with you, and basically interact with the world. I felt a panic attack coming on. My heart started

Factory reset for an attitude adjustment.

to race. Determined, I kept exploring every possible solution to find a fix. No matter how inconvenient, I didn't want to be without my communication device.

As I lay in bed yesterday waiting to start my day, God challenged me once again: "Kim, do your 'internal errors' that manifest themselves as sin bother you? Do you download Scripture to reveal the issues of your heart? Do these issues cause you to be angry, prideful, fearful or judgmental? Would you panic if you lost fellowship with me for month?"

On finishing this blog, my computer glitched again. As the eye gazer rebooted, I realized that I needed a reset, too, after losing my temper earlier that day. Factory reset time once again.

TODAY'S SONG

"Word of God Speak" by Mercy Me

Gospel Graffitti

Written: December 6, 2017

PSALM 25:4–6

Show me your ways, LORD,
teach me your paths.
Guide me in your truth and teach me,
for you are God my Savior,
and my hope is in you all day long.
Remember, LORD, your great mercy and love,
for they are from of old.

This Friday I head back to Augusta for my three-month evaluation. Because we are in the Christmas season, I want to give a gift to each member on my ALS team. My mom agreed to help me try something new: paint simple letters while holding a foam paintbrush with my teeth.

My mom covered canvases with red paint, the ALS Association color. For the next step, I would paint the word "Hope" with my mouth. Comically, I could not see the end of brush on the canvas. Everything close-up looked blurry. Definitely harder than I had anticipated.

So I put on my reading glasses. With the magnification, I often tried to start painting way before the brush touched the canvas. I also had to bite down hard on the plastic handle to keep the brush steady. I completely destroyed that

Pause and consider who God is to you.

paintbrush. When I finished, drool, not paint, covered the towel that lay across my chest. Sorry you missed the show.

Why the word "Hope"? It means more to me than holding my breath until I am healed. So I share with others in their dark moments that God is their hope and their help. We are not alone when we are hurting. God has been using my ALS to draw me closer to his heart, demonstrate his love, and let me have a front row seat to see him at work. I am not going to ever be able to paint pictures that display the greatness of my God. I will stick to gospel graffiti: words that cause you to pause and consider who God is to you.

TODAY'S SONG
"All To Us" by Chris Tomlin

Stay in the Game

Written: December 14, 2017

EPHESIANS 1:3

*Praise be to the God and Father of our Lord Jesus Christ, who has
blessed us in the heavenly realms with every spiritual blessing in Christ.*

I am not a big fan of change. I could maintain the same
routine indefinitely and be perfectly content. Predict-
ability feels safe and comfortable to me. Dealing with the
changes that ALS brings to my life reveals my immature
emotional responses. As a visual learner, if I can't wrap my
head around how things will work, I tend to give up. Techni-
cally speaking, I first freak out then quit.

Several years ago, I wondered if I should stop working. My
ALS had started in my legs, and I increasingly became accident-
prone. Both my safety and recovery time became concerns for
me. I sat in church debating whether to resign. The sermon
encouraged us to take advantage of God's provisions so that
we could continue to serve. So instead of calling my boss that

afternoon to quit, I called Ed, a wounded-warrior friend. He promptly delivered a beautiful candied-apple-red electric scooter for me to use, free of charge.

First a scooter, then a wheelchair, and now a vent.

This last Friday when I met with my ALS team, they suggested that I have surgery to install a vent in my throat. I had failed my breathing test. To be successful, the testing process requires facial muscle coordination, of which I have none. I'd never enjoyed breathing through a snorkel tube, and the thought of breathing through a tube planted in my throat gave me the heebie-jeebies.

I spent hours this week crying and trying to absorb this change. Finally, I accepted God's provision. This time he has not given me a beautiful scooter, a high-tech wheelchair, or a fabulous, modified, wheelchair-accessible van. He has given me a vent to allow me to stay in the game. I'm still not sure how all this will work, but I'm confident that I will continue to see God at work. And, I will have more opportunities to tell you about it.

TODAY'S SONG

"How Many Kings" by Downhere?

Day 38

Joy

Written: December 20, 2017

PSALM 16:11

You make known to me the path of life;
you will fill me with joy in your presence,
with eternal pleasures at your right hand.

$\mathcal{D}$uring the past few years living with ALS, I have come to see words differently. I recently received a painting from one of my daughter's friends. It hangs beside my bed. I look at it every morning while I wait to start my day. Its words challenge me: "In Your Presence There Is the Fullness of Joy."

How often do I pursue fun by looking for joy? Normally I have joy so I can make situations fun. Then it hit me. The only way for me to have joy is to be in God's presence. If I allow anything else to take my attention away from him, I will be unable to experience joy. "Pray without ceasing" is not an option but a must. Communicating with him keeps me in his presence to rejoice and give thanks in every situation.

Rejoice always, pray continually, give thanks in all circumstances; for this is God's will for you in Christ Jesus (1 THES. 5:16–18).

Looking for joy reaps God's presence.

If someone calls 911, the dispatcher stays on the phone with them until help arrives. They offer guidance, support, and comfort. Their presence on the phone is real though their bodies are not physically present. How incredibly more powerful would it be to grasp God's presence? Nothing is too big, disastrous, complicated, overwhelming, disappointing, discouraging, or emotional for him. Who God is, is my fullness of joy. I have a choice every moment of every day to experience joy or not.

My Christmas wish this year is presence rather than presents.

TODAY'S SONG

"In Your Presence" by William McDowell

Day 39

Stray

Written: January 21, 2018

EPHESIANS 2:8–10

For it is by grace you have been saved, through faith—and this is not from yourselves, it is the gift of God— not by works, so that no one can boast. For we are God's handiwork, created in Christ Jesus to do good works, which God prepared in advance for us to do.

A stray dog found its way to our remote country home and overturned our trashcan looking for food. He had apparently been on his own for some time. He has stayed on with us for over a week. We have no cage, fence, or leash. As I grew up, my pet dogs required maximum effort to keep them at home. I had never experienced this type of canine behavior before.

Quasar, "Q" for short, ran after our car when we headed to church last Sunday. We found him waiting on the porch when we returned home. Since then, throughout the day, whenever we open any door to go outside, there he sits. He wags his tail so hard it shakes his whole body. His desire to be loved is precious.

Quasar's insecurity comes not from his lack of name tag, or collar, or papers, or pure bread status, or because he needs a bath. All he knows is that he doesn't want to be left alone.

I desperately want to be with my Master.

God's love for me is boundless. He gives freely, not based on my behavior, status, or accomplishments. My relationship with the Lord started the day I admitted that I needed to be rescued. "Q" reminds me that my Christian service doesn't draw me to the Lord as much as my grateful heart does. I'm an adopted stray. And I desperately want to be with my Master, too.

TODAY'S SONG

"When I Think of Home" by Brian Duncan

Why Them?

Written: January 28, 2018

JONAH 4:2

He prayed to the Lord, "Isn't this what I said, Lord, when I was still at home? That is what I tried to forestall by fleeing to Tarshish. I knew that you are a gracious and compassionate God, slow to anger and abounding in love, a God who relents from sending calamity.

*J*anuary is "Missions Emphasis" month at our church. Each week, different organizations and individuals share how God has been at work. The month blesses and challenges me tremendously. I began to wonder, "Why I have never heard a missionary sermon about Jonah?" God used him to accomplish a huge revival. Three days of pathetic effort resulted in 120,000 lives changed.

Jonah hated the way God overturned Nineveh; he wanted God to handle them differently. Jonah resented God's mercy and compassion toward them. He had contempt for their sin and wanted justice more than he wanted Nineveh to be transformed.

Jonah wanted God to overturn them—in other words, destruction. Ironically, Jonah was the one who needed his attitude overthrown.

What is Nineveh to you?

A friend manipulated and hurt me in college. I decided to avoid anyone similar who could hurt me that way again. I developed a Jonah attitude. The Lord had to overturn me then as well.

The book of Jonah illustrates that a self-righteous heart can be harder to change than an entire city. God asks me to go to my "Nineveh." What sinner, or group of sinners is your "Nineveh?" Will you join me?

TODAY'S SONG

"Let it Start with Me" by No Other Name